Forget-Me-Not

Forget-Me-Not

*A Collection of
Autograph Verses
1880s-1980s*

*Designed and Compiled by Bonnie Hughes Falk
Illustrated by Nancy Delage Huber*

Published by BHF Memories Unlimited
              3470 Rolling View Court
              White Bear Lake, MN 55110

Distributed by Adventure Publications, Inc.
                P.O. Box 269
                Cambridge, MN 55008

Copyright © 1984 by Bonnie Hughes Falk
All Rights Reserved

Library of Congress Catalog Card Number: 84-90501
ISBN 0-9614108-0-9

Printed in the United States of America

To my husband, Tom, and sons, Scott and Andy, for their patience and understanding while I worked on this book.

To my mother, Mae Hughes Kjos, from whom I inherited an interest in preserving the past, for keeping her autograph album tucked safely away.

To John Schell, whose folklore class inspired this book, for his continued support.

To Sarah Stewart Taylor, a special friend, for her advice and enthusiastic encouragement.

ACKNOWLEDGMENTS

I am grateful to the following individuals for furnishing me with autograph albums and for offering me encouragement and support:

Jo Cutler Allen, Marian Anderson, Lois Handwerker Bechtel, Margaret Bezanson, Mariette Bolduc, Michelle Bolduc, Vi Campbell, Merideth Chelberg, Shirley Lockwood Clark, Dr. Nicholas Cords, Blodwen Davis, Grace Davis, Lois Eugster Elton, Florence Evans, Vernelle Sueker Falk, Janice Meredith Fredericksen, Jean Hanson, Barbara Hefta Hoff, Alice Hollingsworth, Anne Huber, Carole Huber, Janet Huber, Selma Hughes, Carrie Kostroski, Sue Krings, Marie Kuharski Kuhnz, Ruth Lang, Elaine Lee, Linda Lee, Peggy MacRae, Brenda Veeder Magnuson, Reba Meixell, Beatrice Miller, Marjorie Andersen Nelsen, Charleen Austin Nelson, Gerry Perrin, Vicki Johnson Peterson, Sharon Philipson, Lois Roberts, Kokila Roche, Dr. Patrick Roche, Sherry Rouse, Norma Schlichter, Shirley Selzer, Barbara Simpson, Barbara Thomas Stalsberg, Shayne Stocker, Elma Wesner Summers, Katie Thomas, Robert Taylor, Elsie Williams, Helen Giannini Zappa, Jim Zappa.

I would also like to pay tribute to all those deceased individuals whose albums were handed down to descendants so that we continue to have a record of the past. Their albums were invaluable in completing this book.

INTRODUCTION

While completing a project for an American Folklore class at Lakewood Community College, I was reminded of an autograph album I had when I was in school. I began asking friends and relatives if they had albums when they were younger and discovered that many of these little books were packed away in trunks, long forgotten. Those who were able to locate their albums (some after hours of searching in the attic) enjoyed recalling former friendships and reliving memories of their youth. I became fascinated with the rhymes and sayings and began jotting them down. So what began as a small project evolved into this collection of verses, all of which were taken from actual albums of friends, relatives, and ancestors.

I have arranged the verses by decades, beginning with the 1880s when autograph albums were in full swing in this country. There is a gradual change from the flowery, sentimental, and often moralistic verses of the earlier decades to the more simplistic, down-to-earth, and often quite cynical verses in the later years. Common topics of the verses included love, marriage, advice, and best wishes. The main theme was friendship, whether expressed in a sentimental, cynical, or humorous way.

The primary owners of autograph albums around the turn of the century were young people in their late teens and twenties. The albums were very ornate, with the verses often written in beautiful Spencerian script. In later decades, young girls of upper elementary and junior high ages were the main owners, with boys frequently contributing verses.

The verses written in autograph albums capture the vitality of our youth, and as they are passed on from generation to generation, they continue to be a source of enjoyment. As you read this collection of verses, maybe you will recall a former classmate you have not seen in years, a favorite teacher, or possibly even your first love!

I have left the 1980s' pages blank so that you may ask your friends to write expressions of their friendship, thereby carrying on the tradition of writing in autograph albums.

ENJOY!

CONTENTS

1880s	Let not the dust of forgetfulness Gather upon the mirror of thy memory.
1890s	May your life be like a piano-- Straight, upright, and grand.
1900s	'Tis only where the shadows linger That the freshest mosses grow.
1910s	Here's hoping your life is like a Ford-- A rattling success.
1920s	May you sail on the ship of fortune And land on the shore of success.
1930s	May your virtues ever spread Like butter on hot gingerbread.
1940s	In your golden chain of friendship, Please regard me as a link.
1950s	May the hinges of our friendship Never rust.
1960s	It takes both the sun and the rain To make a beautiful rainbow.
1970s	There are big ships and little ships, But no ship like friendship.
1980s	Life is an autograph-- Write it well!

The Forget-Me-Not has come to be known as the flower of friendship and fidelity.

Please address comments and inquiries to:
Bonnie Hughes Falk
3470 Rolling View Court
White Bear Lake, MN 55110

COFFEE GRINDER
49¢

1.29 per pair
ELASTIC INSTEP SHOES

SNAP ON HANDLE & IRON
75¢

Let not the dust of forgetfulness

1880s

Gather upon the mirror of thy memory.

*May you, my friend, be ever blest
With friends selected from the best,
And in return may you extend
The gem of love to every friend.*

May no cloud along thy pathway
Ever hide the sun.
May you have a glorious sunset
When life's day is done.

Kind hearts are the gardens,
Kind thoughts are the seeds,
Kind words are the blossoms,
The fruits are kind deeds.

Needles and pins,
Needles and pins,
When you get married
The trouble begins.

*Friendship is a fragile flower
That seldom blooms on earth.
'Tis only nourished by the few
Who realize its worth.*

May happiness crown your days.

Had I the power to carve or paint
Thy future, my dear friend,
It would be fair and ever bright,
Unclouded to the end.

*Go forth this little volume
Like Noah's faithful dove,
And bring to darling Winnie
An olive leaf of love.*

*Long may you live
And have good times.
Marry the chap
That's got the dimes.*

In your chimney of friends,
Please consider me a brick.

Let not our friendship
Like the roses, wither,
But like the evergreen
May it last forever.

Our friendship has budded on Earth,
May it blossom in Heaven.

Your album is a garden plot
Where all your friends may sow.
Where thorns and thistles flourish not
And naught but flowers grow.
I also in your garden plot
Will plant one seed, forget-me-not.

When you are married and have a broom,
Its use I would commend.
In sunshine use the brushy part,
In storm the other end.

*Remember me
When a great way off,
Where the grasshoppers died
With the whooping cough.*

Calico dresses

Saturday nights

I do not wish thee grandeur
Nor yet a store of wealth.
I wish thee greater treasure--
Contentment, peace and health.

White gloves

Sleigh rides

Fruit ripens as it softens,
Love and kisses soon grow cold.
Young men's vows are soon forgotten,
Look out, May, don't get sold.

May your life be like a piano--
1890s
Straight, upright, and grand.

Life is a volume, each year is a page
To be filled up with trophies
From youth to old age.
Let none be more noble, nor womanly true
Than those pure and lovely
Filled yearly by you.

May your life be like the flowers,
Beautiful, blooming and bright,
Fair as the radiant roses,
Pure as the lily white.

Long may you be happy,
Long may you be blessed,
In a neat little cottage
With the one you love best.

Deep as the dark blue ocean,
Pure as the pearls of the sea,
So deep is my heart's devotion,
So pure is my love for thee.

Always do your best;
Angels can do no more.

May you always be happy
And live at your ease.
Get a good husband
And do as you please.

In memory's casket,
Drop one pearl for me.

May the friendship formed in childhood
Blossom in our riper years,
And as time flows on, be strengthened
Whether smiles be ours, or tears.

*To knit and sew
Was once a girl's employment,
But now to flirt and have a beau
Is what they call enjoyment.*

You ask me to write in your album,
I hardly know where to begin.
For there's nothing original in me
Except original sin.

Remember me when all is still
And the moon shines soft on yonder hill,
And the robin sits in the forest tree,
Oh then, dear friend, remember me.

Love me long,
Love me little,
Love me like
An old tin kettle.

Apples are good,
Peaches are better.
If you love me
Answer my letter.

Let each day of your life
Make a beautiful picture
To be hung in the gallery of time.

May happiness ever be thy lot
Wherever thou shalt be,
And joy and pleasure light the spot
That may be home to thee.

None but those who have experience
　Can realize the inconvenience
　　Of riding in an open buggy
　　When the moon shines bright
　　　And the road is muddy.

When I am dead and in my grave
And all my bones are rotten,
This little verse will tell my name
When I am quite forgotten.

May future with her kindest smile
   Wreath laurels for thy brow.
May loving angels guard and keep thee
   Ever pure as thou art now.

Blue waters may between us roll
And distant be our lot,
But if we fail to meet again,
Dear friend, forget-me-not.

Boys are few,
Girls are plenty,
Don't get married
Before you're twenty.

These few lines to you are tendered
By a friend sincere and true,
Hoping to be remembered
When I'm far away from you.

The truest happiness is found
In making others happy.

May the God of Heaven protect you
And keep you from all sin.
When you knock at the golden gate,
May the angels let you in.

*A man of words
And not of deeds
Is like a garden
Full of weeds.*

Roses are red,
Roses are yellow,
And you're the girl
Who stole my fellow.

May your life have just enough clouds
To form a glorious sunset.

*When you get old
And cannot see,
Put on your specs
And think of me.*

May your life be long and happy,
May your death be calm and sweet,
May the angels ever guide you
Till in Heaven we shall meet.

Do not look for wrong or evil,
You will find them if you do.
As you measure your neighbor,
He will measure back to you.

Don't judge your friends by their looks;
Handsome shoes often pinch the feet.

When the golden sun is setting
And your mind from care is free,
When of others you are thinking,
Will you sometimes think of me?

Be unto others kind and true,
As you would have others be unto you.

Never marry a fellow,
Be it lover or brother,
Whose hair is one color
And mustache another.

If wisdom's ways you wisely seek,
Five things observe with care:
Of whom you speak, to whom you speak,
And how, and when, and where.

When your life on earth is ended
And this path no more you trod,
May your name in gold be written
In the autograph of God.

Here's hoping your life is like a Ford--

1910s

A rattling success.

When night pulls down its curtain
And pins it with a star,
Remember you have one true friend
No matter where you are.

In the kitchen washing dishes,
Think of me and my best wishes.
My love for you shall never fail
As long as pussy has a tail.

A wise old owl lived in an oak,
The more he saw the less he spoke,
The less he spoke the more he heard,
Why can't we all be like that old bird?

When you get married
And live upstairs,
For goodness sakes
Don't put on airs.

You are passing through the school of life;
    May you graduate in Heaven.

May you live long,
May you live happy,
May you and your old man
Never get snappy.

May your life be like a snowflake,
Which leaves a mark but not a stain.

If all the luck I wished for you
Were measured out in weight,
I'would have to be tied up in sacks
And sent to you by freight.

When in the tub taking a scrub,
Think of me before you rub.
If the water gets too hot,
Put in a small forget-me-not.

When rocks and hills divide us
And you no more I see,
Just take up pen and paper
And drop a line to me.

When filling memory's woodbox,
  Throw in a stick for me.

Write injuries in dust,
Kindnesses on marble.

True friends are like diamonds--
Precious but rare.
False ones like autumn leaves--
Found everywhere.

May your cheeks be ever rosy
And your heart be ever gay,
When a manly voice shall whisper
"Ruthie, darling, name the day."

When you get married
And your husband gets cross,
Pick up the rolling pin
And say, "I'm boss."

*Choose not a friend
From outward show.
Feathers fly high,
But pearls lie low.*

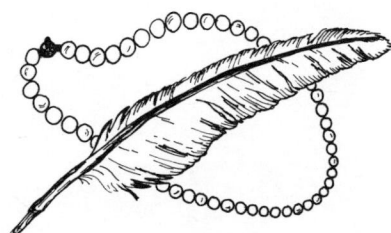

Remember this and bear in mind,
A trusty friend is hard to find.
When you find one good and true,
Change not the old friend for a new.

Green are the leaves,
Green is the vine,
I've chosen you as a friend of mine.
I've picked you out of all the rest,
The reason is I love you best.

There is a pale blue flower
That winds around the shepherd's cot,
And in the silent moonlight hour
It softly sighs, "Forget-me-not."

May all your eggs be fried in grease,
May all your days be spent in peace,
May Heaven's blessings on you flow,
And protect you from a homely beau.

When you are married
And mending britches,
Remember me
Between the stitches.

I won't say, "Remember me,"
'Cause then you wouldn't care,
But I'll turn the verse around
And say, "Forget me if you dare."

As you slide down the banister of life,
  Let me be a sliver in your career.

May your paths be strewn with roses,
  And all your kids have pug noses.

"I draw the <u>line</u> with kissing,"
Said a maiden with firm intent.
But he was a football player
So over the <u>line</u> he went.

When you go out to a party
And don't come home till late,
Remember it is bedtime
So don't swing on the gate.

May friendship consecrate these lines
And memory hold them dear,
And may they oft recall to mind
The hand that placed them here.

"Your teeth are like the stars," he said
Holding her hand very tight.
He spoke the truth, for like the stars
They all came out at night.

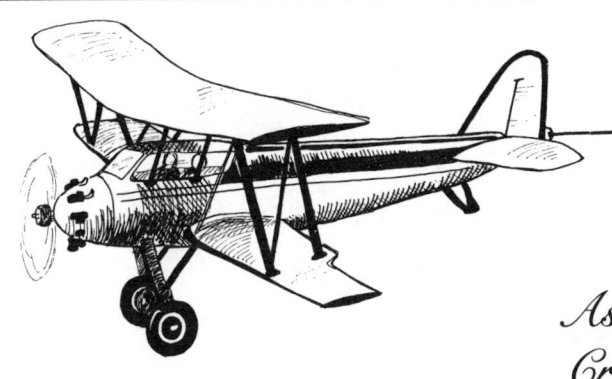

As sure as Lindy
Crossed the blue,
May fortune
Always fly to you.

 *You may fall from a steeple,*
You may fall from above,
But for heaven's sake,
Don't fall in love.

When cupid shoots his arrow,
  Let's hope he <u>Mrs</u>. you.

When you get married,
Don't marry a flirt.
Marry a man
Who can mend his own shirt.

May your married life be sunny,
And your husband fat and funny.

*May your life float
Down the river of time
Like a bob-tailed chicken
On a watermelon rind.*

There was a young man,
There was a young miss,
And on her pink lips he planted a kiss.
That one kiss grew, as little things will,
And from that one kiss he's harvesting still.

I wish you health,
I wish you wealth,
I wish you gold in store.
I wish you Heaven after death,
What can I wish you more?

A little gas, a little oil,
A little spark, a little coil,
A piece of tin, two inches of board,
Put them together, and you'll have a Ford.
Let's go for a ride!

Yours till potatoes wear specs for sore eyes

Yours till they tie horses to the Saturday Evening Post

Pocket full of nickels,
Pocket full of dimes,
House full of kids,
And not one's mine.

Yours till Italy gets Hungary and eats Turkey fried in Greece

Friendship is like old china--
Precious, rich and rare.
When it is broken it can be mended,
But the crack is always there.

When bananas grow on sidewalks,
When the sands of the Sahara are muddy,
When cats and dogs wear B.V.D.'s,
Then I will like to study.

They walked in silence because it was late,
He walked ahead to open the gate,
She wanted to thank him but knew not how,
For he was a farmer and she was a cow!

Some folks don't mind their own business.
The reason is you'll find,
They either have no business
Or else they have no mind.

Mae is your name,
Single in your station.
Happy is the man
Who makes the alteration.

Johnny raised his hand,
The teacher said, "No."
The joke was all on teacher,
Johnny didn't have to go!

Yours till the horse flies

Yours till Niagara Falls

*Cows like lettuce,
Pigs like squash,
Do I like boys?
Yes, by gosh!*

*If ever a husband you should have
And this book he should see,
Tell him of your youthful days
And kiss him once for me.*

Little dabs of powder,
Little spots of paint,
Make a pretty girl
Look just what she ain't.

The moon shines east,
The moon shines west,
But my old man
Makes the moon shine best.

Park your gum here. X   I live by the river--drop in!

I've never been to Harvard,
I've never been to Yale,
But I got my education
In the Minnesota Jail.

In your golden chain of friendship,

1940s

Please regard me as a link.

Oklahoma

Brand new state! Brand new state, gon-na treat you great!

The thing that goes the farthest
Toward making life worthwhile,
It costs the least and does the most,
Is just a pleasant smile.

Peaches grow in California,
They grow in Florida, too,
But it takes a Wisconsin climate
To grow a peach like you.

Yours till the kitchen sinks

Yours till the garden walks

Roses are red,
Violets are blue.
A monkey like you
Should be in the zoo.

Yours till the Mississippi River wears rubber pants
to keep its bottom dry

Some folks say love is like an onion,
You eat it with great delight.
Then you often wonder
Whatever made you bite.

When you get married
And live by the lake,
Please send me a piece
Of your wedding cake.

I love you little, I love you mighty,
I wish your pajamas were next to my nightie.
Now don't be mistaken, don't be misled.
I mean on the clothesline, not in your bed!

The ducks are in the barnyard
Going quack, quack, quack.
Pat is in the park
Going smack, smack, smack.

Down in the cellar
Sitting in the dark
Sat Shirley and her feller
Happy as a lark.

Yours till the Red Sea stops blushing

Forget me not,
Forget me never,
Till all your teeth
Fall out together.

Yours till Prince Albert gets off the can

The two were on the doorstep,
Their lips were tightly pressed.
The old man gave the signal,
And the bulldog did the rest.

Hair is made to hang in curls,
Cheeks are made to blush,
Eyes are made to wink at boys,
Lips are made--oh, hush!

Doesn't it make you mad,
Doesn't it get your goat,
When you jump in the bathtub
And can't find the soap.

Twinkle twinkle little star,
Lois on a trolley car.
If the car runs off the track,
Lois wants her nickel back.

You have a little finger,
You have a little toe,
Now that you're a little bigger,
You have a little beau.

I wish you luck, I wish you joy,
I wish you first a baby boy.
And when his hair begins to curl,
I wish you then a baby girl.
And when her hair is straight as pins,
I wish you then a pair of twins.

Yours till Roy Rogers rides the kitchen range

Yours till the buffalo runs off the nickel

The higher the mountain,
The cooler the breeze,
The younger the couple,
The tighter they squeeze.

Now I lay me down to sleep,
A bushel of peanuts at my feet.
If I die before I wake,
You'll know I died of a bellyache.

Beware of boys whose eyes are grey,
They kiss you once and turn away.
Beware of boys whose eyes are brown,
They kiss you once and turn you down.
Beware of boys whose eyes are blue,
They kiss you once and ask for two.

Papa Moses shot a skunk,
Mama Moses fried a hunk,
Baby Moses ate a chunk,
Holy Moses, how he stunk!

If in Heaven we do not meet,
Hand in hand we'll stand the heat.
If it gets intensely hot,
Pepsi-Cola hits the spot.

*Two in a hammock
Attempting to kiss.
The hammock turned over
and landed like this.*

Yours till the mountain peaks to see the salad dressing

Roses are red,
Violets are blue.
You have a figure
Like a B-42.

Roses are red,
Grass is green.
You've got a figure
Like a washing machine.

Bonnie had a little lamp,
She had it trained no doubt,
For every time her fellow came
The little lamp went out.

Life is like a deck of cards;
When you're in love, it's ♥
When you're engaged, it's ♦
When you're married, it's ♣
When you're dead, it's ♠

When apples grow on peach trees,
When two x two is ten,
When monkeys wear pajamas,
I'll forget you then.

OUQTINVU

You may kiss beneath the lilac,
You may kiss beneath the rose,
But the proper place to kiss
Is just beneath the nose.

A penny a kiss,
A penny a hug,
By the time you get married,
You'll have a full jug!

Yours till Bear Lake has cubs

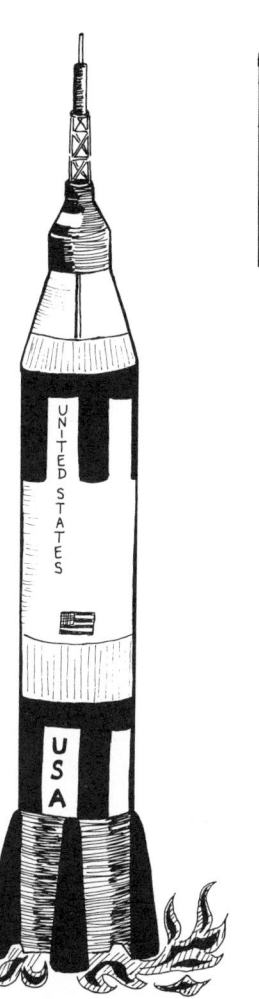
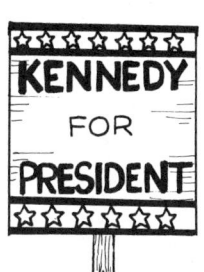

It takes both the sun and the rain

1960s

To make a beautiful rainbow.

You can always tell the English,
You can always tell the Dutch,
You can always tell the Yankees,
But you can't tell them much.

Roses are red,
Violets are blue.
Rain on the rooftop
Reminds me of you.
Drip.
Drip.
Drip.

The finest music in the world,
The sweetest and the best,
Is the music of kind words
In loving thoughts expressed.

I saw you in the ocean,
I saw you in the sea,
I saw you in the bathtub--
Whoops, pardon me!

When you get married
And have twins,
Don't come to me
For safety pins.

When you get old
And out of shape,
Remember girdles
Are $2.98.

Remember the miss
who scribbled this.

2 Ys U R
2 Ys U B
I C U R
2 Ys 4 me

If I were a bunny
With a tail of fluff,
I'd jump on your dresser
And be your powder puff.

Can't think, brain dumb,
Inspiration won't come.
Poor ink, bum pen.
Best wishes, Amen.

If I were a cabbage,
I'd cut myself in two.
The leaves I'd give to others,
But the heart I'd save for you.

*Sailing down the stream of life
In your little red canoe,
May you have a pleasant trip
With just room enough for two.*

Don't make love
By the garden gate.
Love is blind
But the neighbors ain't.

Every clown in town will read this upside down.

Lonesome city,
Dreary state,
Sorry friend,
I forgot the date.

*If you're standing
On a stump,
Think of me
Before you jump.*

What? Write in your book
For critics to spy?
For the learned to laugh at.
No, not I!

There are big ships and little ships,

1970s

But no ship like friendship.

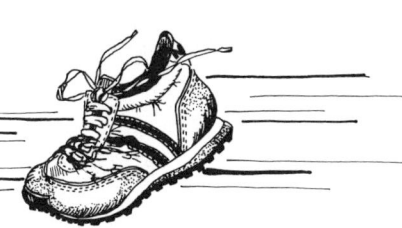

*If all the boys
Were across the sea,
What a good swimmer
Barb would be.*

God made butter,
God made cheese,
God made Debbie
For the boys to squeeze.

*If you see a monkey
Up in a tree,
Don't throw a rock,
It might be me.*

Boys

Boys

Sailors like ships,
Babies like toys,
All that Michelle likes
Is boys, boys, boys.

Boys

Boys

When you are old
And think you're sweet,
Take off your shoes
And smell your feet.

*It makes me giggle,
It makes me laugh,
To think you wanted
My autograph.*

2 good
2 B
―――
4 gotten

2 young
2 go
―――
4 boys

Your name is Susie
And my name is Pat.
You're a real doozy
But I'm a cool cat.

You are my friend,
You are my friend,
You are my friend divine.
Please give me <u>your</u> bubble gum
'Cause you're sitting on <u>mine</u>!

Remember Grant?
Remember Lee?
The heck with them,
Remember Me!

When you get older
And live in a hut,
Send me a picture
Of your first little nut.

Don't B ♯
Don't B ♭
Just B ♮

My ♥  4 U

Roses are red,
The grass is green.
My face may be ugly
But yours is a scream.

By hook or crook,
I'm going to write in this book.

2 friends
----
2 gether
----
4 ever

*If you go to Heaven
Before I do,
Just bore a hole
And pull me through.*

Tu-lips in the garden,
Tu-lips in the park,
But the best tu-lips
Are tu-lips in the dark.

When the golden sun is setting
And your hair has turned to grey,
May you be as sweet a woman
As the girl you are today.

Life is an autograph--

1980s

Write it well!

Way back here
Where nobody will look,
I'll sign my name
In your autograph book.

                Bonnie Hughes Falk